MR.TIMMA

THE STORY OF AN OX...

POOJA S

Contents

CHAPTER I

The Step Towards the Beginning

This is the story of an ox and a girl.

In a small village, a family of four lived together—a father, a mother, and their two daughters. In villages, it's common to see cows tied in the backyard, and people's lives often begin before sunrise: cleaning the yard, collecting cow dung, milking the cows, and taking the milk to the nearby dairy. Their day always starts with the aroma of fresh tea brewed with that very milk.

But this family hadn't kept a cow for many years. One day, they decided to bring one into their lives. Just a village away, they found a calm, gentle cow that was soon to give birth to her first calf. The family brought her home, unaware that fate had just planted the seed of something truly special. They took good care of the cow and fed her very well.

When the sun was red and hiding behind the clouds, the cow wandered off after accidentally getting untied. The father tried to catch her, but she slipped away. That's when the younger daughter, Tridha, stepped in. She followed the cow patiently, gently held the rope tied to her nose, and whispered soft, calming words.

She placed her hand on the cow's head, gently stroking her with care and affection. The cow calmed down under her touch, and Tridha slowly led the cow back home. At that moment, Tridha felt a deep connection with the beautiful soul behind those gentle eyes.

That was the first step towards the beginning of a beautiful friendship.

CHAPTER II

A Magical Arrival

Tridha was in the city, staying in a hostel while attending college. One evening, while returning from class on a crowded bus, her phone buzzed, and her eyes lit up excitedly. It was a picture of the cow... and beside her, a newborn calf—a baby boy.

Her heart swelled with joy and warmth. She couldn't wait to meet him. That weekend, when Tridha returned home. Her sister greeted her with a wide smile and said, "The cow gave birth in the open field, right on our land. Father carried the little one in his arms. Everyone was so happy and celebrated his arrival that day."

Together, they hurried to see the calf. They found him sitting calmly in the shade when they arrived, his eyes twinkling like tiny stars, and his ears were large, giving him the appearance of Lord Ganesha.

There was an aura of peace around him—almost magical—as if he had brought a little piece of heaven down to earth.

The little calf began to explore the world through his curious, bright eyes. His days were simple, yet filled with warmth and peace. He would sleep soundly, and when he woke, he'd drink milk from his mother, then drift back into peaceful slumber.

Everyone in the family adored him, especially his mother, the cow, who was his greatest protector. It was astonishing to witness the depth of her love. She never let him out of her sight. No matter where he lay, she stood close by, enveloping him in her warmth, making sure he was always safe and cherished. The bond between them was a beautiful display of a mother's love.

And the calf had his playful side, too. When the family milked the cow, they always milked him first. After he had his fill, they would begin milking. During that time, the calf quietly observed with his large, innocent eyes, eagerly waiting for the last few drops of milk.

This was his small world—filled with love, warmth, and simple joys.

CHAPTER III

The Little Adventure

One quiet afternoon, the calf was resting peacefully in the yard. His mother was nearby, grazing behind a fence. The sun was gentle, and the air was still — it felt like any ordinary day.

But suddenly, the calf stirred. He opened his eyes and saw his mother just beyond the fence, calmly munching on fresh grass. Without a second thought, he tugged at the thread tied to him. Once... twice... again and again — determined and surprisingly strong for his size. Then, with a bold spark of will, he broke free.

He ran straight toward the fence!

In a hurry, he didn't notice the sharp edges and squeezed through the narrow gap. The rough fence scratched his soft neck, leaving red marks across his tender skin. But he didn't stop his little heart carried only one thought — to reach his mother, and he did.

He walked up to her gently and began to drink her milk, just like always. Tridha's mother, noticing the empty yard, rushed out in worry. But what she found made her pause. There he was, standing beside his mother, peacefully feeding. Her concern turned into a smile, and tears welled in her eyes at the courage of someone so small and the love that made him fearless.

This little adventure was just another part of his story.

CHAPTER IV

A Name and A Bond

As the days passed, the little calf quietly made his way to the hearts of the family. With his lazy routines—sleeping, drinking milk, and nothing more—he became everyone's favorite in no time.

They decided to name him Timma—a name as soft and endearing as his nature. It suited him perfectly, with his slow steps, sleepy eyes, and calm, adorable presence.

Among them all, the younger daughter, Tridha, shared the most special bond with Timma. She would sit beside him for hours, gently rubbing his head until he drifted to sleep.

And Timma, clever in his sweet way, had figured out how to keep her close.

Many a time, he would pretend to be fast asleep—eyes closed, breathing slowly—so she wouldn't get up. He loved her warmth, gentle voice, and her presence beside him. But the moment she shifted slightly to leave, thinking he was asleep, he'd peek through one eye, lift his head, and stand up like he'd never slept.

Such a little actor he was—fooling her to keep her by his side a little longer.

There's also a process to help a calf shift from milk to grass. In the beginning, Timma refused everything except milk. But Tridha's mother, with patience and love, would bring him tender green grass every day, placing it gently in his mouth and teaching him to chew. Slowly, he began to enjoy it—first fresh greens, then dry hay.

Timma was no longer just a calf in the house. He was family—a quiet bundle of joy, innocence, and mischief wrapped in love.

CHAPTER V

Growing Together

As the world paused during the COVID-19 lockdown, with schools and colleges closed, Tridha returned home and began attending online classes—and in that unexpected quiet, she found a new friend in Timma.

They spent their days together—walking in the fields, playing under the trees, and sitting quietly as the sun set. In him, she found laughter, peace, and a little brother. In her, he found love and a friend.

As time passed, Timma began to grow. Slowly, he stopped drinking his mother's milk and started grazing, learning to eat grass on his own.

Every morning, as Tridha woke up and stepped outside, her eyes would search for one face—Timma's. The calf would be tied just outside the house, waiting under the early sun.

She would call out cheerfully, "Hi Timma!"

At the sound of her voice, Timma would perk up, look around, and then tilt his head upward to catch a glimpse of her on the balcony—as if saying, "I'm here!" She would come running downstairs, wrap her arms around him, and plant a kiss on his head. It was their special start to the day.

Timma, as everyone knew, was a foodie. All he ever wanted was food! Tridha's mother made sure he had plenty—fresh grass to munch on, water to drink, and all the care a calf could need.

After finishing her online classes, Tridha would take Timma out to graze. But he was not an easy calf to manage. The moment he was untied, he would leap with joy and run wild across the land—nibbling grass from every corner, jumping, turning, full of playful energy.

Taking him out was easy. Bringing him back? That was a whole other story.

Timma never wanted to stop eating. So, Tridha had to get creative.

She'd take a bundle of grass and walk ahead, waving it in front of him like a little bribe. Timma, curious and hungry, would follow, running behind her with his eyes locked on the green bundle.

Sometimes, he'd get upset, especially when she didn't immediately give it to him. He'd stop and stare at her. But soon, his stubbornness would melt away. He'd forgive her and patiently follow her again, trusting the bundle would come to him.

On sunny days, Tridha had another trick. Since the grazing land was near their home, someone from the family may be her mother or sister, would fill a bucket with water and make a sound, splashing or tapping it. Timma, hearing that familiar signal, would come running all the way home, eager for a cool drink.

And just like that, through little games, simple love, and shared habits, Timma came home, every time.

CHAPTER VI

Where's Timma ?

One sunny afternoon, Tridha tied little Timma to a nearby plant and ran home quickly to drink some water. She thought she'd be back in just a minute. But when she returned, Timma was not there.

Her heart skipped a beat.

She called out, "Timma! Timma!" but there was no sound, no movement. She searched all around. Finally, in the middle of the field, between tall green plants, she saw a little movement.

There he was — hiding perfectly in the middle of the field. His height matched the plants so well that he was nearly invisible. But the moment he saw her, his tail flicked and ears twitched, as if he'd been playing hide-and-seek all along.

Timma was a lovable soul. No matter how much grass surrounded him, if Tridha offered him just one little blade from her hand, he would take it with joy. He loved to eat from her hand, sitting beside her like a child glued to his best friend.

Days turned into weeks, and weeks into months. Timma was growing. He was no longer a tiny calf, but a little brother to the young girl.

No matter where he was, if she called, "Timma!" he would stop whatever he was doing — eating, sleeping, playing — and come running to look for her.

She loved to tease him. She would hide behind a wall and call his name. On her Call, Timma would stop chewing, lift his ears, and slowly peek around the corner — as if playing detective. If she were upstairs, he would look up and search for her on every balcony.

But of course, Timma's love always came with a hunger. After all the games, the peeking, and the searching, he would eventually nudge her gently, asking, "Where's my grass?" Always the foodie!

CHAPTER VII

A Day of Worry

One day, something felt different. Timma wasn't in his usual energetic self. His body felt colder than normal, and he seemed a little too quiet. Earlier that day, the family had eaten watermelon and given him the outer rinds to chew on.

But after eating them, he suddenly sat down — and didn't get back up for a while. His head drooped to the side, and his eyes looked sleepy. It wasn't his usual lazy nap — something felt off. The family grew anxious. Everyone stopped what they were doing, gathered around him, and watched closely, hoping it was just a momentary spell.

He didn't play, didn't munch, didn't even ask for grass. The whole day passed with worry hanging in the air.

But by evening, Timma was back on his feet — slowly moving around, giving a soft "moo," and finally nibbling some grass. The family sighed in relief. After that day, they decided not to feed him watermelon rinds anymore, no matter how much he might ask for them again.

Timma also had his little habits — and his little demands. He refused to drink plain water unless some cow feed was sprinkled into the bucket.

If they forgot, he'd stand near the bucket and nudge it with his nose, giving a look that said, "Should I knock this over?" Sometimes, he'd even pretend like he was about to tip it over, just to get attention.

when Tridha's mother added a little feed, he would drink with a sense of victory

That was Timma. A little dramatic, a little spoiled — and completely loved.

CHAPTER VIII

A New Little Sister

Days passed in joy, laughter, and growing friendship. Timma was now a part of every moment in the family's life.

And then — a new surprise arrived. The cow gave birth again — this time, to a beautiful little calf, a girl. Timma had a little sister!

The family tied the newborn calf next to Timma, thinking he would welcome her sweetly. But Timma had other plans.

When no one was around, he would slowly turn toward her and give her his big, wide-eyed stare — not exactly a warm welcome, but more like a playful scare. His sister, still tiny and new to the world, would get startled and shuffle back.

But the moment someone came by, Timma would instantly turn innocent. He'd blink slowly, act calm, and look around as if nothing had ever happened.

One day, he was caught red-handed. Tridha's mother went quietly and saw the whole scene — Timma staring wide-eyed at his sister, and the little calf shaking slightly in confusion. When he realized he was caught, he quickly turned his face away, pretending to be deeply interested in a patch of grass nearby.

That was Timma — full of mischief, but never without love.

Even though he teased her, deep inside, he was slowly learning how to be a big brother. His world had grown a little bigger — and a lot more fun.

CHAPTER IX

A Fearful Goodbye

The family had grown — the cow, Timma, and now his little sister. They were a little herd of three, living peacefully with the family.

But the world outside was changing. In the past, oxen were the pride of every farmer, used to plough fields and carry heavy loads. Now, machines had taken over. Tractors had replaced oxen. Those who had them would sell them — sometimes to good farmers, but too often to people with cruel intentions.

And then there was Timma. Three years had passed since he came into their lives. He had become a part of the family — like a son, a little brother. But as he grew, so did the effort of feeding him, especially during harsh summers or heavy rains when grass was hard to find.

People around them began whispering.
"If he were a cow, at least it would've given milk."
"There's no use in keeping him, he's of no value."
"You won't be able to feed him much longer. Better give him away now."

But Tridha and her family didn't see Timma as a burden. He was family, not just livestock.

One day, a man from a nearby village came. He said he had another bull that matched Timma's size and strength. If they gave Timma to him, he would train them as a pair to plough the land.

The girl's heart sank. She didn't want to give him away. She begged her family not to agree. She fought back, pleading, "He's not just a calf — he's my friend. My Timma."

The man said he would return on Friday evening to take him.

The girl spent the whole week in fear, counting down the days with a heavy heart.

And then Friday came. Evening arrived... and passed. But the man never showed up. Later, her father gently told her, "I told him not to come. I said, 'My daughter won't give away her Timma.'"

Relief washed over her like a wave. Tears mixed with laughter as she ran to Timma, hugged him tightly, and kissed his forehead. That day, she took him out to graze with even more love in her heart. Timma was still hers.

For now, the family was still whole.

CHAPTER X

Bigger, Wiser, Timma

Time moved on, and so did Timma.

He had now grown as tall as Tridha — a gentle giant with the same innocent heart. He had grown up alongside her, and their bond was unbreakable.

On special days, the family would perform a small pooja. Tridha would bathe him, scrubbing his back gently while he stood still, blinking slowly like he enjoyed every second of it. She'd colour his horns and put a tilak on his forehead. In those moments, he looked like a divine being — calm, glowing, and graceful.

Even now, he would rest his head on her lap. His horns had grown bigger, so Tridha had to be careful. Now also his love never changed. One single call — "Timma!" — no matter where he was, he would come searching for her with is eyes sparkled, like they held a thousand stories.

And yes, he was still a foodie. But he never made a call, even when he was hungry or thirsty. He wouldn't moo or make a fuss. He would simply stand like a statue, looking at the house, patiently, silently waiting for someone to notice, and the family always did.

Because they understood him. They knew his silence, his stillness. They read the language in his eyes and in the way he stood. They knew when he wanted water, when he wanted food, when he just wanted a little company.

Timma had grown in size, in calmness, and wisdom. But in their hearts, he was still the same little calf who once pretended to sleep on a warm lap, just to hold on a little longer.

CHAPTER XI

The Weight of Letting Go

As seasons changed, so did life. Darkness began to creep in — not into their hearts, but into the everyday struggles. It was monsoon time, and the rain poured endlessly. The green grass, which Timma loved so much, became harder to find. The land was drenched, the fields muddy, and there was barely enough grass to feed him.

Still, the family didn't give up. Day after day, they walked through the rain, cutting whatever grass they could find from nearby lands. The elder daughter would carry the bundles on her head, soaked and shivering, but determined. Tridha, using her scholarship money, brought more dry grass. They did everything just to see Timma and his family eat in peace.

But the world outside didn't change. People began to speak again.

"Why are you still keeping him?"
"Isn't it enough? You're making your family suffer for this animal."
"You're being stubborn. Just let him go."
Their words were harsh and constant. And slowly, the pressure started to crack Tridha's brave heart.

One evening, with her eyes brimming with tears and her throat tightening with pain, she whispered —
"Okay... give him away. But only to a family who will love him... and care for him... like we did." Her words were soft, but they carried the weight of the world. She had held on for so long, through summers and rains. But now, she was tired. Not of Timma — never of Timma — but of the world.

Her eyes were wet. Her voice, trembling. Her heart — shattered, but still loving.

CHAPTER XII

Stolen in Silence

Timma grew stronger and taller, people began asking for him — some to use for ploughing, others with darker intentions. The family was clear and firm: "We've raised him with love. If we ever give him away, it will only be for good—only for honest work, never for harm."

Then one day, a farmer came. He spoke gently, said all the good things. "I'll use him for ploughing. He'll be safe, well-fed. Treated like our own." He convinced the father. The family hesitated, but the weight of feeding Timma, the pressure from outside, the endless struggles — it all added up.

The mother cried. Tridha wasn't home — she was in college, now that the lockdown had ended. They took Timma away in an auto that day.

As Tridha had told her family earlier, "If you ever have to give him away, do it when I'm not home. I don't dare to say goodbye."

The family stood silently, their hearts aching as they watched him go. But they told themselves he was going to a good home — to a safe place, to a future where he'd be cared for.

To ease Tridha's heart, the family requested the farmer to send a picture of Timma once he reached his new home.

But then something strange happened. The farmer stopped answering calls. Hours passed. Messages were left unread. The silence grew heavy.

And then — a twist they never expected.

A Family Friend saw Timma tied along with other oxen, stood confused, quiet, still. He immediately called the father, "Why is Timma here, tied up with animals meant for sale or worse? I thought you said you'd never give him away for bad deeds."

The father was shocked. He couldn't believe it. The truth hit like a slap.

The man who promised to plough the fields had traded Timma away, behind their backs, without a word. The family collapsed into grief — the mother weeping, the father furious and broken. They had been betrayed.

The love they gave, the promises they made — thrown away. But they didn't tell Tridha.

She was still at her hostel, believing Timma was safe, eating grass under a warm sun, maybe even making new friends. Her heart rested on that belief. Because how could they tell her? That the friend she raised like a brother... was now lost to the very world she feared most?

CHAPTER XIII

Timma's Rescue

Love is not silent when it sees betrayal, and this time, the father decided to fight back. With fire in his heart and pain in his voice, he called the farmer again and again, who had broken their trust.

"Return Timma to us. If you don't, we will take legal action. We'll involve the authorities — even bigger people, if needed. You promised one thing and did another. We'll give back your money. We'll pay the auto charges too. But give us Timma. We only want him back."

There was no begging. Only determination!

And finally, after hours of pressure and phone calls, they agreed. Timma, who had been taken nearly 70 kilometres away, was brought back. Weakened, silent, and shaken.

When he got down from the auto, his eyes were sunken and sad. He hadn't eaten properly in two days. But the moment his hooves touched familiar ground, he ran home. Straight to the place he called his own. To the people who had never stopped loving him.

The family's tears melted into relief. The mother rushed to feed him fresh green grass. The father poured clean water into his bucket. Timma, tired but safe, slowly began to eat again.

A short clip was sent to Tridha — still in her hostel — of Timma munching grass. She blinked in disbelief.

He came back...?

They told her everything later. Tridha smiled through her tears.
And soon, the entire village was talking — "Timma is back!"

His return had become the talk of the town. A story of fate, love, and a family that refused to let go.

CHAPTER XIV

The Return of the King

Life slowly returned to normal. Timma, who once came back home weak and afraid, now stood strong again. Whenever he was scared or anxious, he wouldn't let anyone near him, except Tridha.

Her voice gave him strength. Her presence gave him peace.

Timma returned to his kingly routine: eating, drinking, sleeping, and making everyone around him fall in love with his innocence.

One sunny afternoon, after eating a bit too much, Timma lay down in his favourite spot. This time, he didn't curl up — instead, he stretched all four legs out like a sleepy child, enjoying a feast-induced nap. Just then, someone walking by saw him from a distance and panicked.

"Something wrong with Timma!" they screamed.

Tridha heard the voice and came running. "Timma! Timma!" she called. And just like always, Timma slowly opened his eyes, lazily lifted his head, and stood up, half-asleep, his belly full, his legs wobbly. He blinked at her as if to say, "Why the drama? I was just enjoying a nap!" Everyone laughed.

Because that was Timma — the sleepy king of the house, the heart of the family. And when he stretched out like that, it only meant one thing: he'd had the best meal of the day.

Tridha also learnt that cows will not eat and digest like humans. They will store their food and chew it later, slowly, peacefully. And it was Timma who taught her that.

CHAPTER XV

A Final Goodbye

Life, no matter how kind, always tests the heart.

Bringing grass once again became a struggle. Tridha had returned to the city for her studies, only visiting on weekends. The family, busy with farming and daily work, found it hard to care for three cows. They were doing everything they could, but it was becoming too much.

One day, a family friend visited. He had always known Timma's story — the bond, the return, the love. He looked at the family and said gently, "I'll take care of him. I have a coconut plantation — there's plenty of green. My children also do farming. He'll never be alone."

As he was not a stranger. He was someone trusted, even Tridha knew him. She thought long and hard. And then, with a heavy heart, she agreed. Not because she wanted to — but because Timma deserved the best.

Tridha, who always thought cows don't have emotions — they simply eat, sleep, and make sounds for no reason. But it was Timma who changed her heart.

He showed her that cows have beautiful souls. They look up to humans with trust, love, and care.

And they don't call out without reason. They speak when they are hungry, thirsty, or when something happens around them. They speak because they feel.

But due to the limitations of life and the inventory of machinery, thousands of oxen are losing their lives.

And Timma... He wasn't just a calf. He was a companion, a friend, a little brother. in his silence, he taught a young girl the language of love.

• • •

About The Story

Timma

Growing up in the village of Dasanapura in Mysore district, Karnataka, I witnessed the pure and beautiful bond between people and their Cows. This close and caring connection deeply inspired me to write this story. It reflects the harmony, warmth, and innocence of rural life.